Mega Watt

J.J. Watt's Surge to Greatness

Kristie Rieken

TRIUMPH
BOOKS

Library of Congress Cataloging-in-Publication Data

Names: Rieken, Kristie.
Title: Mega Watt / Kristie Rieken.
Description: Chicago, Illinois : Triumph Books, [2015]
Identifiers: LCCN 2015041617 | ISBN 9781629372433 (paperback)
Subjects: LCSH: Watt, J. J., 1989– | Football players—United States—
   Biography. | BISAC: SPORTS & RECREATION / Football. | TRAVEL /
   United States / South / West South Central (AR, LA, OK, TX).
Classification: LCC GV939.W362 R54 2015 | DDC 796.332092—dc23
LC record available at http://lccn.loc.gov/2015041617

This book is available in quantity at special discounts for your group or organization. For further information, contact:

Triumph Books LLC
814 North Franklin Street
Chicago, Illinois 60610
(312) 337-0747
www.triumphbooks.com

Printed in U.S.A.

ISBN: 978-1-62937-243-3

Design by Patricia Frey
Cover Design by Andy Hansen

Photos courtesy of AP Images unless otherwise indicated.

Contents

1 | The Making of Mega Watt

Watt a Start

The life of the man who would one day become an adopted Texan and one of the state's most popular and famous residents began more than 1,100 miles from Houston in the Milwaukee suburb of Waukesha, Wisconsin.

Justin James Watt was born on March 22, 1989, in Waukesha. He was a big baby and weighed almost 10 pounds at birth. Watt grew up in nearby Pewaukee, Wisconsin—a small town of about 13,000 people. He was raised by his parents, John—a firefighter—and Connie Watt. Early on it looked like hockey might be his sport, and he played it from age 4 to 13. But football soon took over as his true love.

He appeared in a newspaper article when he was seven and was asked who his favorite player was. Below the picture of a towheaded Watt was his answer: "Reggie White. He's a good football player. They played really good on Monday night. I want to be a football player."

His mother has often talked about her son's lifelong affinity for sports, and has said he developed his love for football when he was in fifth grade. John worked 24-hour shifts 11 days a month as a firefighter. On days when he wasn't at work, he'd be outside with J.J. and his other sons, Derek and T.J., tossing a football or playing catch.

"When I have kids, I will try to model everything I do after my parents, John and Connie," J.J. said in a story on the University of Wisconsin website. "They drove me to the hockey rink early in the morning and late at night. They took me all over the country playing sports. But they also harped on me in the classroom, harped on me to be a good student, harped on me to be a good citizen, and harped on me to be a good friend."

By high school J.J. Watt had developed into a multiple-sport star. He was a four-year letterman in football but also lettered in basketball, baseball, and track in his time at Pewaukee High School. He was a first-team All-State selection in track after becoming a state champion in the shot put his senior year.

Watt started as a backup quarterback early in his high school career but wasn't a very accurate passer, so he settled in as both a tight end and a defensive end. He earned first-team All-State honors on offense and defense and was named the team's MVP as a senior. On defense he piled up 44.5 tackles for losses, including 18 sacks in his career, and had 38 catches for 549 yards and 11 touchdowns on offense.

The well-rounded Watt was also a member of the National Honor Society and made the high honor roll.

A fresh-faced Watt, wearing 99 for the Wisconsin Badgers.

Not the Right Decision

Despite his stellar high school career, Watt was only rated a two-star recruit by both Rivals.com and Scout.com. When he began fielding scholarship offers he was already 6'5" but weighed only 220 pounds, not yet having filled out what would one day be his massive frame. Still, there was a decent amount of interest in Watt, but not at the level one would expect for someone who would go on to be a two-time NFL Defensive Player of the Year.

Watt pursues the play against the Indiana Hoosiers at Camp Randall Stadium on November 12, 2010.

His stock was partially hurt by a bout with mononucleosis the summer before his senior year, which kept him from attending any college camps. Despite his illness, he received scholarship offers from Wyoming, Northern Illinois, Minnesota, Colorado, and Central Michigan. Watt had loved Wisconsin since he was a child and had worn Badgers gear from the time he was a toddler. But Wisconsin did not offer him a scholarship, and he committed to Central Michigan, which had offered him a full scholarship. "I just wanted to play football," he said. "It didn't matter to me where."

Watt reconsidered his decision to attend Central Michigan after Coach Brian Kelly left the school to coach at Cincinnati, and instead verbally committed to Minnesota to play for Coach Glenn Mason. But Mason was fired before Watt signed, and the future NFL standout ended up back with Central Michigan after meeting new coach Butch Jones and liking the things he had to say about how the tight end would be used in his system.

But it quickly became clear that things weren't going to work out the way Watt had envisioned. He started as a tight end and appeared in all 14 games as a freshman, but he caught just eight passes for 77 yards.

"I wanted to play in the NFL. I wasn't going to do it catching eight passes in the MAC [Mid-American Conference]," Watt said. "I knew I had to make a change. I looked at my parents and said, 'This isn't what I signed up for.' A lot of kids would be very happy being a starter on a Division I football team, but I wanted more and I wanted to play in the NFL, and that was my dream. I kind of took an all-or-nothing shot."

There were other factors too. He wanted to be close to his tight-knit family and longed to play defensive end again.

Watt left school in December 2007, after football season, and had to figure out what to do next. He received his release from Central Michigan and applied to and was accepted at Wisconsin; his parents would be on the hook for his tuition this time. Watt then got permission from then–Badgers coach Bret Bielema to walk on to his team. But that wouldn't be until the fall of 2008, which left several months to kill.

He filled that time in a way that has helped build his legend. He spent six months delivering pizzas at the Pizza Hut in his hometown while earning a few credits at a community college. It certainly wasn't the greatest time of his life. "It was a real humbling experience," he said while at Wisconsin. "Some of the little kids who once looked up to me [when I played in high school] would answer the door and say 'Mom, why is J.J. Watt here?' And the only thing I could say back was, 'I have your pizza.' It was real humbling. And it brings you back to earth real quickly."

But he wasn't simply delivering pizzas and attending a couple community college classes during this time. He was working out like a madman. He weighed just 245 pounds when he left Central Michigan. By the time he began practicing at Wisconsin he had bulked up to a whopping 285 muscle-bound pounds.

At Long Last a Badger

After years and years of loving Wisconsin, Watt finally became a Badger in 2008. His first season at the school wasn't at all glamorous. Watt redshirted that season and worked with Wisconsin's scout team. Yet he attacked that task with the same fervor he now shows in games, and was named the team's Defensive Scout Team Player of the Year. He went so hard in practice that he sometimes annoyed the scholarship players he was supposed to be helping.

His work impressed the coaching staff so much that he was awarded a scholarship in the spring of 2009, a relief after taking the gamble of walking away from his full ride at Central Michigan. In 2010 Watt talked about a conversation he had with Bielema about attaining a scholarship:

"I said, 'What do I need to do to earn a scholarship?' And he said, 'You need to be in the two-deep and that will earn you a scholarship.' And I said, 'I'll be there by the end of my first year.' We didn't know where—I was playing d-tackle and d-end, there was even talk of me playing tight end as well—but I played everywhere and I ended up on the defensive line and loved it and just relentlessly worked my tail off to earn a job and earn a scholarship."

Watt was a starting defensive end for the Badgers by the beginning of the 2009 season. His debut came on September 5 in a win over Northern Illinois in his first game in almost two years. It was a glimpse of what Watt would one day be. He had six tackles and half a sack, and swatted down a pass.

He showed a knack for getting into the backfield early in his career at Wisconsin and had four and a half tackles for losses in his first five games. He had a breakout game against Iowa on October 17 when he had a season-high eight tackles—four for losses—including a sack. Watt also toiled on special teams that season and was named the team's co–Special Teams Player of the Week after he blocked a field goal against Michigan on November 14.

Watt had another big game that season, against Hawaii on December 5, when he

Watt intercepts a Michigan pass; Big Blue eats dust.

had three backfield tackles—including two sacks—and a quarterback hurry to earn Big Ten Defensive Player of the Week honors. But perhaps his best game of the season came in a win over Miami in the Champs Sports Bowl on December 29. He had three tackles—two for losses plus a sack— knocked down two passes, and recovered a fumble to star in that game.

He ended the year second on the team in tackles for losses (15.5), pass breakups (5), and fumble recoveries (2), and his 4.5 sacks were third on the squad.

In 2010 Watt reflected on how much Bielema meant to his development: "I can't be more thankful for Coach B. for just trusting in me and believing in me that much," Watt said. "I've seen people… criticize him all over the place, but you can't argue with his results. It's unbelievable."

After such a solid performance in his first season at Wisconsin, everyone was eager to see what he'd do for an encore. Watt didn't disappoint. In the 2010 season opener against UNLV on September 4, he broke up a career-high three passes, had half a sack, and forced a fumble that was returned for a touchdown.

Watt's season only got better from there. He had three tackles for losses, plus two sacks, to help the Badgers knock off then–No. 1 Ohio State 31–18 on October 16,

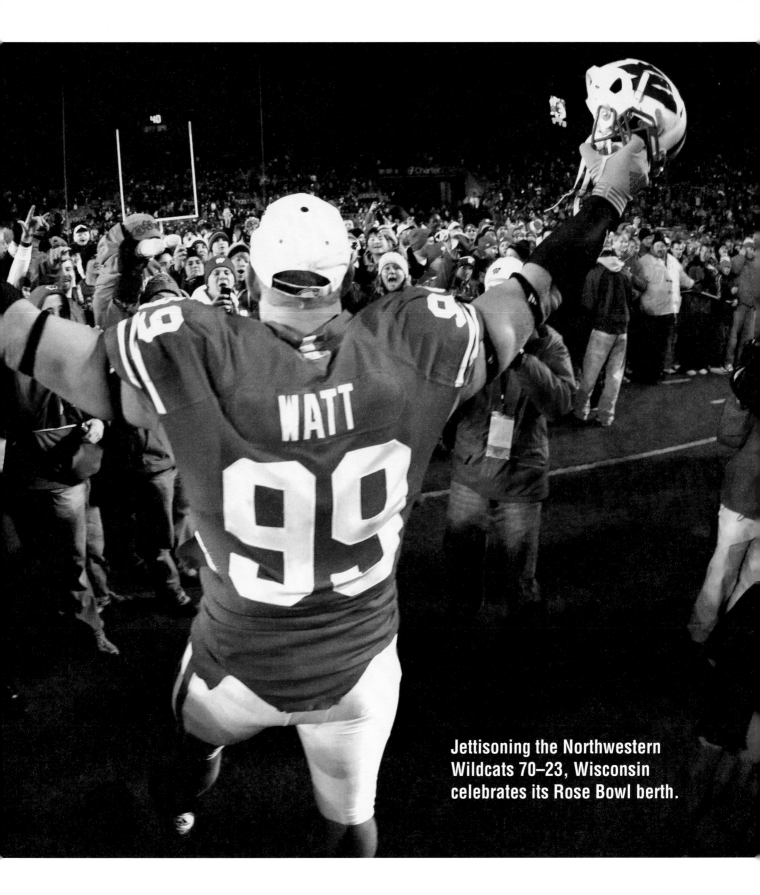

Jettisoning the Northwestern Wildcats 70–23, Wisconsin celebrates its Rose Bowl berth.

Headed into the bowl game against TCU, a confident Watt faces the media.

2010. A week later he was instrumental in giving Wisconsin a 31–30 win over Iowa. He had two tackles for losses and a sack in the game and earned multiple honors for the week after blocking an extra point in the one-point win.

He added another line to his already impressive stat sheet by grabbing his first career interception in a win over Michigan on November 20. A week later, in the regular-season finale against Northwestern that gave the Badgers a share of the Big Ten title, Watt was at his best, again earning Big Ten Defensive Player of the Week. He had seven tackles in the game, including three for losses, and forced two fumbles. He also had three quarterback hurries, all of which led to interceptions by Wisconsin. The crowd chanted his name in the third quarter when he blocked an extra point attempt. "We needed to bring a title back to Wisconsin, and that's exactly what we did," he said after the game. "And we couldn't be happier."

The Badgers reeled off seven straight wins to cap the regular season to rise to No. 4 in the polls and earn a trip to the Rose Bowl against third-ranked TCU. "I've seen everything, from the bottom of college football to the top of college football," Watt said in the week leading up to the Rose Bowl. "Now I'm playing in the Rose Bowl. I never dreamed it would turn out like this. I'm playing for my Central Michigan buddies. I'm playing for every college player who doesn't have the chance to do this." Watt had three tackles and broke up a pass in the 21–19 loss to the Horned Frogs.

Watt led the team that season with 21 tackles for losses and earned first-team All–Big Ten honors, was voted a second-team All-American by both the Associated Press and *Sports Illustrated*, won the Lott IMPACT Trophy, and was named the team's MVP for his work during the 2010 season.

It would be his last year with the Badgers; after careful consideration, Watt decided to forego his senior year and declare for the NFL Draft. "It's always been a dream of mine to play in the NFL, just like every kid," Watt later said at the combine. "I felt like I had a very solid year, and the opportunity presented itself for me to make the jump to the next level. And you don't get many opportunities more than once—I learned that in my experience so far."

After Watt made the difficult decision, Bielema raved about the work he had done for his team: "As a defensive end and overall as a defensive lineman, I've never had anybody better," he said. ★

Watt earned the Ronnie Lott IMPACT Award, which is given to the player nationwide who has the biggest impact on his teammates off the field.

2 | Unpopular Draft Pick

Draft Analysis

Watt received an invitation to the 2011 NFL Scouting Combine after declaring for the draft following his successful, albeit short, career at Wisconsin. To say he turned in an impressive performance at the annual evaluation of top-level prospective NFL talent would be an understatement. Some have called his workout one of the top 10 most eye-popping offerings in the history of the combine.

Watt was measured at 6'5" and 290 pounds on combine day. He ran a 4.84 40-yard dash, bench-pressed 34 reps of 225 pounds, and had a 37" vertical jump and a 10' broad jump.

He was given a draft grade of 8.37 out of 10 by NFL.com. In their evaluation of Watt they noted that he was hardworking, intelligent, and a relentless player. "Good height, fast hands, and great anticipation allow him to bat down a ton of passes," the evaluation continued. "Watt will give you everything he's got and is certainly a first-round selection."

Knowing what is known now about Watt makes their evaluation of his weaknesses almost laughable: "Won't consistently get the edge on tackles with his get off or quickness," it read. "Plays high at times, can be blown off the ball by the double team, but does fight hard to hold ground. Lacks some lateral mobility both rushing the passer and playing in space. Will occasionally give up outside contain."

Despite any criticism of his potential, Watt was supremely confident in his ability and what he could bring to whoever drafted him. In a video leading up to the draft he talked about his best qualities. "I'm tenacious and a relentless defender," he said. "I feel like I would be doing a disservice to the game of football and all of the fans if I didn't go 110 miles an hour all the time."

So why did he think a team should draft him? "I'm going to work harder than everybody else in the film room, the weight room, and on the field," he said. "I'm going to lead your football team. I'm going to be one of the best defenders in the National Football League, and I'm also going to be an ambassador for your team off the field."

No. 11

Ten players were selected in the 2011 NFL Draft before Watt heard his named called. Some of those men turned out to be good players, and some are even great, but it would be hard to argue that any are better than Watt.

1. The top overall pick was quarterback Cam Newton, who went to the Carolina Panthers. The Heisman Trophy winner

started every game as a rookie and earned AP Offensive Rookie of the Year honors. He's a two-time Pro Bowler who has started all but two games in his four-year career.

2.   Texas A&M linebacker Von Miller was the second pick and first defensive player chosen when he was drafted by Denver. Miller was the AP Defensive Rookie of the Year and has been selected to the Pro Bowl three times and was named

an All-Pro in 2012. His career took a detour in 2013 when he was suspended for the first six games of the season for violating the NFL's drug policy.

3.   Alabama defensive tackle Marcell Dareus went third, to the Buffalo Bills. He's been a steady performer, starting all but one game in four seasons, earning two Pro Bowl trips, and being named an All-Pro in 2014.

Watt displays his power during agility drills at the 2011 NFL Scouting Combine in Indianapolis.

4. The Bengals went with offense with the fourth pick and chose Georgia receiver A.J. Green. He excelled from the start and is a four-time Pro Bowler who has had at least 1,000 yards receiving in each of his NFL seasons.

5. LSU cornerback Patrick Peterson went fifth, to the Arizona Cardinals. He has also proven to be a good choice, making the Pro Bowl in each of his first four seasons and being named All-Pro twice. He's also a punt returner, and scored four touchdowns on returns as a rookie in 2011.

6. Alabama receiver Julio Jones went to the Falcons at No. 6. He's a two-time Pro Bowler who had a career-high 1,593 yards receiving during the 2014 season.

7. Missouri's Aldon Smith was snagged by San Francisco with the seventh pick. His career got off to a promising start, and he was named to the Pro Bowl and was an All-Pro in 2012 after finishing second to Watt with 19.5 sacks. But Smith was felled by off-the-field trouble and was released by the 49ers in August after his fifth arrest in three years.

8. The Titans took Washington quarterback Jake Locker with the eighth pick. Locker started 23 games in four seasons for Tennessee before retiring in March 2015.

9. The Cowboys used the ninth pick on Southern California offensive tackle Tyron Smith. He has become a stalwart on their offensive line, playing right tackle as a rookie before switching to left tackle in year two. He has started all but one game in his four-year career and has been named to the Pro Bowl twice and was an All-Pro in 2014.

10. The last player selected before Watt was Missouri quarterback Blaine Gabbert, who was taken by the Jaguars. He was mediocre in two seasons as a starter for the Jaguars and was traded to San Francisco in 2014, where he became Colin Kaepernick's backup.

No One Has Higher Expectations for Me Than I Do

When Houston finally made Watt an NFL player by taking him with the 11th overall pick in the 2011 draft, Texans fans weren't exactly overjoyed.

People in the Lone Star State didn't know much about this guy who was once a pizza delivery driver. Some complained the team should have taken Auburn defensive tackle Nick Fairley, who was the SEC Defensive Player of the Year in 2010, or Nebraska cornerback Prince Amukamara, a unanimous All-American.

When the official Twitter account of the Houston Texans announced that the

A beaming Watt holds up a No. 1 Houston Texans jersey. He was Houston's first pick, and the 11th overall.

team had selected Watt, the majority of the comments were negative. Many fans simply tweeted "boo" with an excessive amount of *O*s to express their displeasure. One wrote, "Not a good decision," and another tweeted, "Not a wise pick." Other fans tweeted, "HORRIBLE" and "another stupid choice."

The Texans liked Aldon Smith, but thankfully for them he was gone by the time their pick came up. With Watt's selection, the Texans had chosen a defensive player with their first-round pick seven times in eight seasons.

Defensive coordinator Wade Phillips couldn't stop talking about Watt's size and opened his introductory press conference by discussing it. "I think a lot of you are probably saying the same thing: 'Wow, I didn't know he was that big,'" Phillips said, beaming.

He was thrilled to add Watt to a defense that already featured defensive end Mario Williams, the top overall pick in the 2006 draft. Phillips was wowed by Watt's impressive performance at the combine.

"Running as fast as he did, and as quick as he is, all those things plus his size and mobility, those aren't okay statistics," Phillips said. "This guy is a really good athlete. I think he's humble, which we really like about him, but this guy is as good of an

athlete that was up there. I think all of us will see that."

Watt was well aware of how fans felt about him and wasn't daunted by the negative reaction. "That's fine," he said, before flashing a huge smile, the day he was introduced in Houston. "I've heard there have been some disappointed people, and that's fine with me. I've been doubted before, and Coach Phillips and the coaches here all have confidence in me, and I have confidence in myself as a football player. At the end of the day, that's all that matters. If the coaches believe in me and if I believe in myself and the team, we're going to be just fine."

During a teleconference just moments after he was drafted, Watt was asked about the pressure of living up to being a high draft pick. His answer provided a glimpse into the personality and temperament of the future star. "No one has higher expectations for me than I do," Watt said. "I am going to come in and give it everything I have, and at the end of the day, I hope it helps the team win football games, because that is what it's all about."

When Watt was drafted, the Texans, who started as an expansion team in 2002, had never made the playoffs. A big reason for that was the dominance of

NFL commissioner Roger Goodell congratulates the league's newest addition.

Displaying his new jersey No. 99, Watt poses for the press with his new coach, Houston defensive coordinator Wade Phillips.

Peyton Manning and the Indianapolis Colts in the AFC South, in which they'd won seven of the last eight division titles. During the teleconference the night he joined the Texans, Watt was asked if he'd be open to playing inside if that's where Phillips decided he'd work best. "I feel very comfortable playing anywhere along the defensive line," he said. "The goal is to sack Peyton Manning. That's what everyone around here is saying. That's my job."

That night Watt was already licking his chops at the thought of taking down not only Manning, but any other quarterback in his path. "That's definitely the goal of a defensive end is to sack quarterbacks," he said. "To me it doesn't matter what number or jersey they are wearing. I want to get them all. That should be the mentality of all defensive ends—that you want to sack every quarterback you play. That is the goal."

At the end of the call Watt, then 22, reflected in his circuitous journey to the NFL. "That was always the goal and the dream," he said. "I worked every single day toward it, but the feeling I had today I could have never imagined. It's an unbelievable feeling, and words can't express how I feel. Glad to be a Texan."

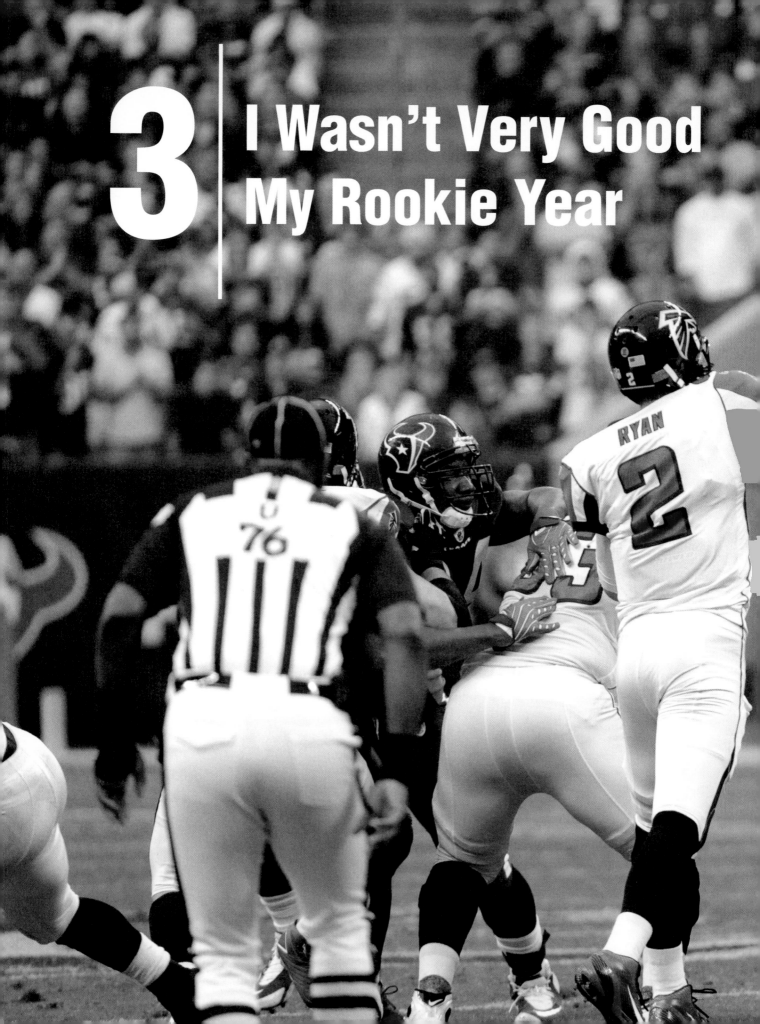

3 | I Wasn't Very Good My Rookie Year

Getting His Feet Wet

Watt had worked his way into the starting lineup by Houston's first game of 2011. In the days leading up to his NFL debut he wasn't anxious, only excited.

"If I go out there nervous or scared, I'm not going to have any success, and this team can't have me playing scared or nervous," he said. "I'm just going to go out there and do what I've been doing my whole life: play the game of football, fly around and have fun...I'm not going to let my first play be memorable for the wrong reasons. I'm going to try to make that one special."

The Texans hosted AFC South rival Indianapolis in the season opener, and Watt got to work almost immediately, taking down running back Joseph Addai after a three-yard gain on third down to force a punt on the Colts' first drive. But that was a pretty routine play.

Watt's first memorable moment came later in the quarter when QB Kerry Collins (not Manning, who would miss the entire season) coughed up the ball and Watt pounced on it, recovering the fumble and returning it two yards to give Houston the ball in the red zone. The Texans went on to win that game 34–7, and Watt finished with five tackles.

It wasn't until Week 3 against the Saints that Watt collected his first sack.

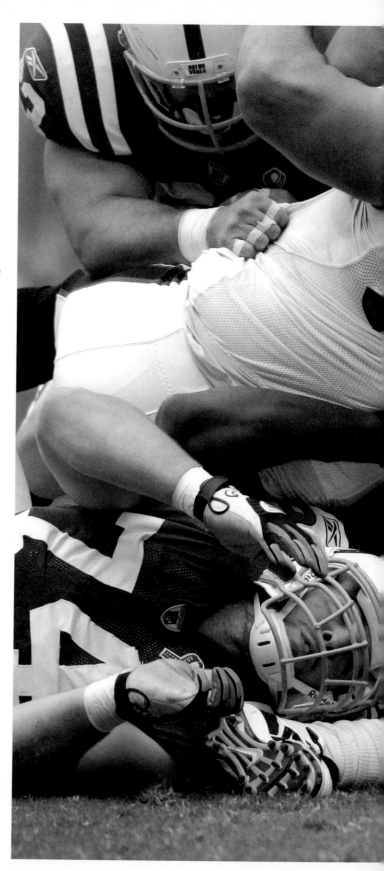

The newly minted NFL star makes an immediate impact, pressuring Colts quarterback Kerry Collins to fumble the football in the Texans' first matchup of the 2011 season.

New Orleans was driving late in the second quarter when Watt chased down Drew Brees and sacked him for a nine-yard loss.

He didn't do much in the next two weeks and had just one tackle in both those games. He reflected on what he was going through at the time in August 2015:

"Early in the season I wasn't very good my rookie year. I was pretty poor as a football player. The thing I was doing was I was trying to do everything perfect. I was trying to take every step perfect. I was trying to place my hands perfect. I was trying to do everything exactly how the playbook said I should do it. When in reality, sometimes you have to go out there and let your instincts take over. Let yourself play football."

Diving In

It took Watt a while, but he finally got out of his head, stopped worrying so much, and got back to being the player that got him to the NFL. In August 2015 he said of the adjustment:

"I just kind of came in one day and said, 'You know what? Screw it. I'm just going to play football the way I know how to play football. I'm going to make mistakes, and that's fine, but I'm going to go out here and I'm going to play the game the way that I feel like it should be played and the

way that I'm proud of playing it.' From there on, it just kind of grew into what it is today. I still make mistakes to this day. I'm always going to make mistakes. It's just minimizing those mistakes and making sure that you try and take calculated risks."

By the middle of the season Watt had improved and Houston's defense ranked first in the NFL. He recovered a fumble in a win over Cleveland in Week 9 before getting the first multi-sack game of his career in his 11th game by taking down Blaine Gabbert twice in a victory at Jacksonville.

His work in this stretch helped Houston reel off a franchise-record seven straight wins despite losing both starting quarterback Matt Schaub and backup Matt Leinart to injuries. Third-string quarterback rookie T.J. Yates took over in Week 13 and won his first start before orchestrating a key drive that capped the seven-game winning streak and gave the Texans their first-ever playoff berth. They trailed when he threw a six-yard touchdown pass with two seconds remaining to give Houston a 20–19 win over Cincinnati. Watt had four tackles, including one for a loss in the big win.

The Texans dropped their last three regular-season games, but it was during that time that Watt began to show flashes of the game-changing ability he now displays.

Watt dwarfs Saints quarterback Drew Brees during game action on September 25, 2011.

Perhaps his best game to date came in his first prime-time matchup, a 19–16 loss to the Colts. Watt had five tackles, including a sack, and swatted down three passes.

But he also made some rookie mistakes, and was called for two penalties on a drive that helped Indianapolis put the game away. "The last two were absolutely unnecessary on my part," Watt said. "That's on me. I can't do that. I can't hurt our football team like that."

Still, the Texans won their first AFC South title and Watt finished the regular season with 16 tackles and led the team with 13 tackles for losses. He also had 5.5 sacks and swatted down four passes.

Making Playoff History

It had been a long and excruciating wait for the Texans to finally reach the playoffs. They began as an expansion team in 2002 and toiled for more than nine years before stepping onto the field for their first postseason game on January 7, 2012.

They still had Yates, the third-string rookie, at quarterback, and on the other side of the ball was Watt. He hadn't lived up to the high expectations he had for himself in the regular season. But everything was new, and it was time to take things to another level and help make history for his young team. Texans fans,

Pittsburgh Steelers quarterback Ben Roethlisberger can't escape Watt's clutches.

who initially weren't pleased when he was drafted, had started to warm up to Watt by playoff time. But he was still virtually unknown out of the confines of Texas. That would begin to change by the end of the day.

The sellout crowd, which had waited so long for this moment, was loud and more raucous than Reliant Stadium had ever seen. There was an electricity in the stadium air before a down was even played.

The game was tied at 10–10 late in the second quarter when Cincinnati rookie quarterback Andy Dalton dropped back to pass. As the ball left Dalton's hands, Watt fought off a block by Mike McGlynn and leapt into the air. He extended both his huge hands skyward and with one mighty swat grabbed his first career interception.

The already wild crowd was brought to a deafening frenzy as the massive defensive end shed a would-be tackle by McGlynn and rumbled 29 yards for a touchdown that put Houston ahead for good.

"I was really just trying to put my hands up and get in the way of the passing lane," Watt said. "It happened to kind of stick. I realized I had the ball so I just ran to the end zone just trying not to fall down."

When he crossed the goal line, Watt held the football in his right hand and saluted the fans with his left. His teammates reached him seconds later and knocked him to the ground in glee. He continued to grip the football as he tumbled down in a mass of joyous celebration. "That was a game changer," head coach Gary Kubiak said.

Watt was the sixth defensive lineman, and first rookie, to score a touchdown on an interception return in postseason history, excluding the Super Bowl. Dalton could only shake his head as he watched it replayed on the stadium's video boards. "He jumped up and made a play," Dalton said. "It was a great job on his part."

Players and coaches on both sides agreed that Watt's play shifted the momentum of the game. "It [was] kind of a big dagger for us," Bengals coach Marvin Lewis said. "We never really overcame it."

Watt didn't top that play during the remainder of the contest, but he did continue to contribute to what became a tough game for Dalton. On the drive after the touchdown, Watt crashed into the backfield and sacked Dalton for a loss of seven yards to end the first half. Then Dalton threw two more interceptions after halftime to help the Texans cruise to a 31–10 victory.

The defensive lineman scores his first NFL touchdown, intercepting a pass against the Cincinnati Bengals in the January 2012 Wild Card Playoff.

The Texans traveled to Baltimore a week later to play the Ravens with a trip to the AFC Championship Game on the line. Watt had a season-high 12 tackles and 2.5 sacks to lead another stellar performance by Houston's defense. But this time it was the Texans' rookie quarterback who made multiple mistakes that foiled the team. The Texans committed four turnovers, including three interceptions thrown by Yates, and their season ended with a 20–13 loss.

The playoff experience left Watt hungry to help the Texans do even more in the future. "You get a little bit of a taste and you're not satisfied with what you got," Watt said. "So now you want to go back and get the whole thing." ★

Watt pumps up the crowd after his first-ever pick 6.

A young fan cheers on the new star.

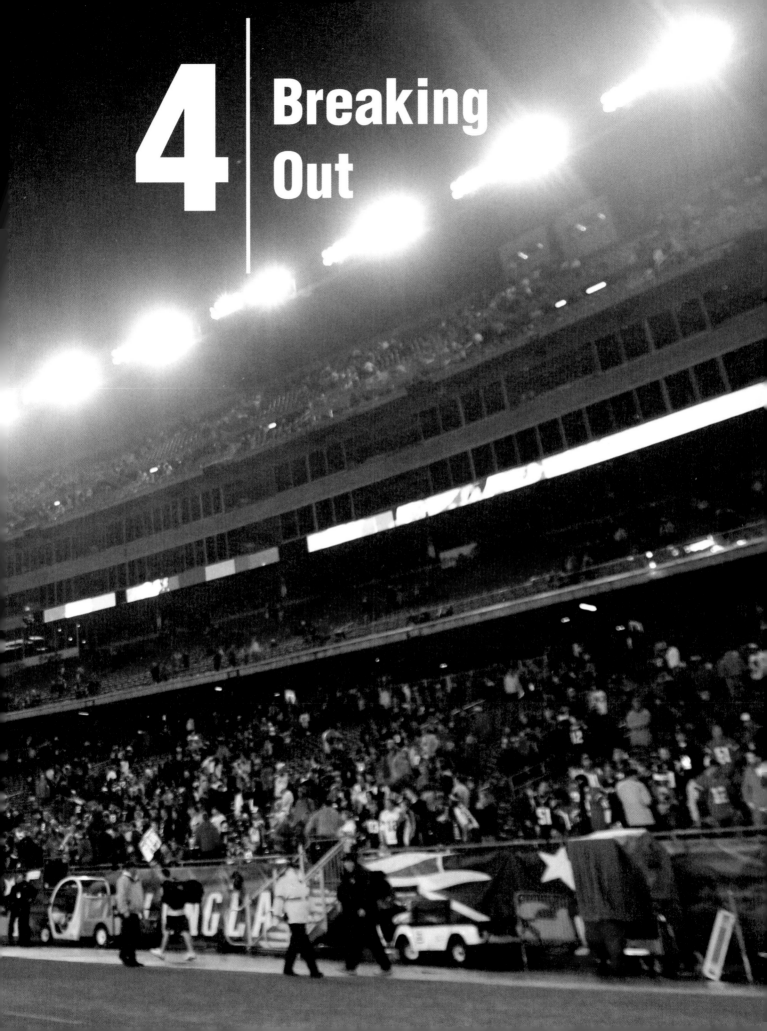

4 Breaking Out

Let's Get Going

Watt's big performance in Houston's first playoff run brought high expectations for him and the Texans as they prepared for the 2012 season. And it wasn't only outsiders who were looking for more from Watt. His teammates challenged him to do more too.

"I expect J.J. to be a megastar," veteran defensive end Antonio Smith said just before training camp began. "But he can't fall off. I told him that this year people are going to be looking for you, you're not going to surprise them anymore, and they're going to get up to play because of your reputation. And it can only go two ways with that: either fall off or become a megastar."

While flattered by Smith's comments, Watt deflected attention away from himself and to the entire defense. "Hopefully that's the case, because that means I'm playing well. That means our team is winning, because you can't become a star without your team winning," Watt said. "I hope our whole defense becomes megastars. We deserve it."

Watt reflected on the growth he'd made in his first year and noted that he knew "how to pass rush way better than [he knew the previous] year." He also felt better equipped to deal with the rigors of the long NFL season with a year under his belt.

He worked hard training in the off-season and added about eight pounds to his already massive frame while becoming both faster and stronger. Watt was happy with the way he had played in spurts as a rookie but looked to become a more consistent player in his second year. Watt said he didn't have a singular pass-rushing style in 2011 but had "honed in [on] one style" as he prepared for his second year.

Watt dislocated his left elbow and missed most of training camp but was healthy and ready to go in time for the season opener on September 9 against the Dolphins. It was clear from the start that Watt was just fine. He had half a sack and deflected three passes, two of which were intercepted by the Texans, in a 30–10 win.

He didn't slow down after that, recording multiple sacks in each of the next three games—all wins by the Texans—to give him 6.5. He'd already surpassed the 5.5 sacks he had as a rookie—with 12 games to go.

His stellar play was rewarded when he was named AFC Defensive Player of the Month for September. But he didn't spend

Watt sacks Dolphins quarterback
Ryan Tannehill in the 2012
season opener.

Broncos quarterback Peyton Manning eats turf too.

much time celebrating the award. "It's an honor, but it's October," he said. "It's a new month, new opportunity. There are much bigger goals out there than Player of the Month."

While Watt wouldn't pat himself on the back for what he'd done, defensive coordinator Wade Phillips was more than happy to praise the work of his star defensive end. "He certainly had a tremendous month," Phillips said. "I've had Reggie White and Bruce Smith and Elvin Bethea and Curley Culp. I've been around a lot of good players, and I don't know that they had any better four games than what he's had."

The Texans improved to 5–0 with a 23–17 win over the New York Jets. Watt was at it again in that one, finishing with a sack and swatting down three passes, including one Houston intercepted. But the victory came at a cost as star middle linebacker Brian Cushing suffered a season-ending knee injury, putting even more pressure on Watt to lead the defense.

A week later the Texans lost for the first time, 42–24 to Green Bay. Watt had two sacks playing in his first professional game in his home state of Wisconsin, but the Packers were simply too much for the Texans.

Six in a Row

The Texans shook off that first loss and regrouped to prepare for a rematch with the Ravens, the team that had knocked them out of the playoffs in January. By that point Watt wasn't a secret to anyone, and coaches around the league feared what he might do to their offenses.

Baltimore coach John Harbaugh raved about Watt in the week leading up to the rematch and revealed that he "loved him in the draft" and enjoyed meeting the big fella during that process. "He's playing exactly the way we thought he was going to play," Harbaugh said. "He's big. He's got great hands, great strength, natural football instincts. He gets his mitts on so many balls it's just incredible."

Watt didn't have a sack that week against the Ravens, but his swatting skills gave Houston a major boost in the 43–13 blowout. The highlight of the game came when Watt swatted a pass by Joe Flacco into the hands of Texans cornerback Johnathan Joseph, who returned it for a touchdown to put Houston up 16–3 in the second quarter. Watt wasn't done yet, and added to his highlight reel when he batted a Flacco throw to the ground in the third quarter.

It was the first of six straight wins for the Texans in which Watt continued to lead the defense. He was solid in all those wins, but perhaps his best game came in a Thanksgiving Day victory over Detroit. He finished with a season-high three sacks and swatted down two passes in the 34–31 overtime win. Watt set the tone for that game by taking down Matthew Stafford for a seven-yard loss on the game's first play.

The Texans clinched their second straight playoff berth with their next win, a 24–10 victory over the Titans. Watt had a sack and batted down two passes in that game to give him 15.5 sacks and an NFL-record 15 passes defended for the season. That put him with Hall of Famer Reggie White as the only players in NFL history to have at least 15 sacks and 13 passes defended in a single season. One of his swats against the Titans led to an interception, and he forced the first fumble of his career when he jarred the ball from Chris Johnson in the second quarter.

Back to the Playoffs, and Some Hardware

By the last quarter of the 2012 season some regarded Watt as the best defender in the league. As Houston prepared to play the Patriots that December, Coach Bill Belichick raved about Watt. "He's the most

Watt gathers steam against the division-rival Tennessee Titans.

Watt goes sky-high in Houston's October 8 game against the Jets at the Meadowlands.

disruptive player in the league, certainly that we've seen," Belichick said. "That looks like the Defensive Player of the Year to me."

Watt appreciated the compliment from such an esteemed coach and talked about the mind-set he has every time he sets foot on the field. "That's what they're paying me to do, to be disruptive and try to be the best in the league," he said. "I've always said all along, if your goal is not to be the greatest, then you're kind of wasting your time. I'm going out here every single day trying to be my greatest."

Of course it wasn't only outsiders that appreciated Watt's work. Phillips, the defensive coordinator, thought he should be considered for league MVP, not just Defensive Player of the Year. "I don't have any doubt that he should be [MVP]," Phillips said. "He's already setting records right now, and we're not through with the season."

The Texans won just one of their final four games in 2012, but Watt was huge in that victory. He had a season-high 10 tackles and tied a career best with three sacks to help Houston clinch its second AFC South title with a 29–17 win over the Colts. Watt also forced Mewelde Moore to fumble on the Houston 1 to keep the Colts from scoring early in the second quarter. "I don't even know the stats," Kubiak said

The defender shows off his lighter side during the October 12, 2012, game against the Baltimore Ravens. The Texans won the game 43–13 and cruised to 6–1.

after the game. "But it seemed like every time I looked up, he was making a play."

Watt finished the regular season with a franchise-record 20.5 sacks to lead the NFL and become the ninth player in league history with 20 or more sacks in a season. He set an NFL record for defensive linemen by batting down 16 passes. Watt led the Texans with 107 tackles and forced four fumbles with two recoveries. He was named AP Defensive Player of the Year, gaining 49 of the 50 possible votes, with Von Miller getting one vote. Watt was also a first-team All-Pro and was voted a starter in the Pro Bowl.

Gary Kubiak was asked what he thought of Watt's breakout year at the end of the regular season. "You are watching something special," Kubiak said. "I don't think you're really going to know that for about 10 years. Watch him play and let him go through his career. If you probably went and broke down what's happened over a period of the first two years in the league for a player, I'm not sure many guys can put up some of the numbers he's put up."

His teammates were in awe of his work too. Star receiver Andre Johnson was impressed by his athleticism. "When you draft players you never know how they'll turn out," Johnson said. "You never know what you're going to get. I guess we hit the gold mine with J.J."

Houston wrapped up the regular season with a franchise-best 12–4 record and drew Cincinnati in the wild card round of the playoffs once again.

Watt was all over the Patriots, but it wasn't enough to stop New England's march to the Super Bowl.

In the week leading up to that game against the Bengals, everyone wanted to talk about Watt's big interception return for a touchdown that helped the Texans win the year before. Everyone that is, except the man himself. "I will not talk about it," Watt said. "That was last year. This is this year, and I have things to focus on this year. It was a great play, huge moment in my life, but I'm looking forward to making bigger moments this year."

Marvin Lewis knew his team would have to find a way to slow Watt down if they hoped for a different result this time around. He even got creative in looking for a way to do that. "I wrote a letter to the commissioner to petition for 13 [players]," Lewis joked. "I figure if we put a guy on each side of him and a guy in front of him, we've got a good opportunity."

The Texans hosted the Bengals on January 5, 2013, and another sellout crowd packed the stadium to see just the second home playoff game in franchise history. Starting quarterback Matt Schaub, who had missed the playoffs a year before, was solid in his first career postseason game, and Arian Foster ran for 140 yards and a touchdown. Watt didn't have a spectacular play like he did in the previous postseason game against the Bengals. But he led the defense with five tackles, a sack, and two passes defended to help the Texans to a 19–13 win.

Next up was a rematch with the Patriots, who had beaten Houston 42–14 the previous season, on December 10. Watt was asked about the pressure of people expecting him to be great in every game. In usual Watt fashion, he answered the question just how you'd want the star of a franchise to respond to such a query. "If you want to be the best you have to want to do things that have never been done before," he said. "I'm always striving to do that. I think if people expected good from me and not great, I would be disappointed. You want people to expect greatness from you."

Watt had half a sack and four tackles in the AFC Divisional Playoff Game, but Tom Brady and the Patriots ran over the Texans in a 41–28 win.

After such a dominant second season, some wondered if it would be the ceiling for Watt. "I'm 23 years old," he said. "I'm still learning what I'm doing out there…. I have a lot of time left in this league, I hope, and I have a lot of improvement to make. My second year is not going to be my best year in the NFL, I promise you that." ★

5 | J.J. Swatt

How Big Are Those Hands?

Watching Watt tackle is cool. Seeing him make a tackle for a loss is even better. Witnessing him chase down a quarterback and throw him to the ground on a sack can be jaw-dropping. But none of those feats come close to how amazing and borderline majestic it is to see Watt stretch out his long muscular arms, stick out his huge hands, and swat down a pass at the line of scrimmage.

He does it so often he makes it look easy. It certainly is not. His ability to swat down passes is like nothing the NFL has ever seen. He's knocked down 37 since entering the NFL in 2011. No defensive lineman in the history of the league has as many.

It's such a unique and impressive skill that it caused Texans fans to nickname him J.J. Swatt early in his career. They hold flyswatters and make signs with renderings of hands batting down footballs. And the most rabid of those fans say they're a part of a fan club called the Swatt Team.

Watt, however, isn't very keen on the clever play on his name. "I'm not a huge fan of it," he said. "I like my last name, and so I don't like that people mess with my last name, but I understand it, I understand why it's a big deal, so that's cool. But I like

The lineman attempts to bat down a pass by RG3 on September 7, 2014.

to honor my grandparents and everyone, so I like my regular last name too."

But he can't help but enjoy some of the creative ways fans pay tribute to his swatting skills. "I appreciate it, and the signs are cool and the big hands in the stands, and all that comes with it—the Swatt Team, the whole deal," he said. "The fans are great. I love what they do, and any way they support me, I appreciate it and accept it."

There are many factors that contribute to his ability to bat down balls. A big one is the size of his hands. At the combine the hands of every player are measured. The number comes from the distance from the tip of the pinkie to the tip of the thumb of an outstretched hand. So just how huge are those hands that Watt uses to knock down ball after ball? They're a whopping $11\frac{1}{8}$ inches. That's right—his hands measure almost an entire foot across. They're some of the biggest hands the NFL has ever seen.

Those mitts are impossible to miss. His hands are so gigantic that moments into his first press conference in Houston, defensive coordinator Wade Phillips grabbed Watt by his left wrist to hold up one of them, showcasing its expanse to the assembled media. Phillips then bragged that he had the largest hands at that year's combine as an embarrassed-looking Watt chuckled.

Combine that with an 82.5" wingspan and a 37" vertical jump and what you get is a quarterback's worst nightmare.

Learning to Swat

Watt is so adept at swatting down passes that it has become second nature. But he didn't perfect the skill overnight. It took many years of practice and film study to make it look so effortless.

His huge hands and long arms certainly play a large role in his success in batting passes, but there's much more to it than that. He started to work on the skill during his redshirt season at Wisconsin. It was then that he met defensive line coach Charlie Partridge, who made teaching linemen to bat down balls his pet project.

"We'd have the d-linemen focus on the quarterback's eyes as they were working to gain ground and then set up and throw the ball and have them work on trying to bat the ball down," Partridge said. "You combine that just with some emphasis points while he's developing, and obviously the fact that J.J.'s pretty special talent-wise."

Though knocking down passes is undoubtedly a crowd-pleaser, Watt prefers to make other kinds of plays. After all, if he swats down a pass, it means he didn't get a sack, which is what he strives for

Watt zeroes in on his latest victim, Joe Flacco.

every time. Batting down a ball is sort of a consolation prize to him. "I know I have long arms," he said. "You can't get a sack every play, so you might as well try to bat the ball."

Watt hasn't forgotten the lessons he learned so many years ago and said when he's rushing he doesn't even look at the line. "My eyes are always on the ball," Watt said. "I know what my hands need to do. I know where my feet need to go. So as I'm pass rushing I can see if [the quarterback's] getting ready to throw."

He has to time his jump perfectly in order for it to work. Often self-deprecating, Watt likes to joke about the times that he doesn't get his hands on the ball. "There's plenty of times where I put my hands up and I look like a fool because the ball's not even close," Watt said. "But you just throw your hands up in the air and hope to get lucky, and obviously I've been luckier than most."

Perfecting the Swat

Watt learned the swat at Wisconsin, but he perfected it in Houston. Bill Kollar, who was the defensive line coach for the Texans from 2009 to 2013, worked extensively with Watt and the rest of the defensive line on the skill.

"You won't hear too many other d-line coaches that say a batted ball is the same thing as a sack," former Houston outside linebacker Connor Barwin said. "We continue to hear that for years now, and I think guys remember and think about that when they're out there rushing the quarterback and they see they're not going to get there, they remember to put their hands up. You'd be surprised how much you can hit the balls down when all you have to do is put your hands up."

As Watt got better and better at batting down passes, teams started using various devices in practice to try and mimic what he could do. Some used brooms, and the New England Patriots once used racquetball racquets to help Tom Brady prepare for Watt.

"The passes defensed is an amazing statistic," Brady said. "You have to know where he's at on every single play because he's so disruptive with tackles for loss and his penetration of the backfield."

By 2012 everyone in the NFL knew that Watt would try to swat down passes, but no one knew how to stop it. Houston's game against the Jets in 2012 was televised nationally on ESPN. After Watt batted down his third pass of the night, their microphones caught a bit of bravado from

It's not just his reach;
Watt can jump too.

the star. "You can't try throwing over my head," Watt yelled at the Jets.

He'd also started wagging his finger after every play where he knocked down a ball, as a warning that people shouldn't throw his way. It's similar to the gesture former NBA star Dikembe Mutombo made after he blocked a shot. Mutombo, whose 3,289 career blocked shots are second in NBA history to only Hakeem Olajuwon, jokingly told Watt that he should pay him royalties for using his signature move.

After his performance against the Jets, Coach Rex Ryan thought he might do well in an NBA uniform too. "J.J. Watt's the real deal," Ryan said. "You would think the Knicks would pick him up, too, with all of the shot blocking he did. It's not like he doesn't do it to everybody, but he certainly did it tonight."

Though he'd heard about Watt's swatting skills and watched film on it, Baltimore coach John Harbaugh didn't realize just how impressive it was until he

In celebration of the NFL's Salute to Service, Watt shows off his own lethal weapons.

Fans know it,
opponents know it.

saw it live. He said they had to adjust their game plan to account for it.

"You really can't believe it until you see it," he said in 2013. "I don't think we really had a great understanding of it last year until we experienced it, what a force he is…. When they get blocked, they all get hands up and they try to find the quarterback's eyes and intentions, and try to get a hand up in the passing lane. He just happens to be the best at it because he's just so big and athletic."

Watt believes batting down passes is demoralizing to quarterbacks. He sees their body language change when they think they've found a receiver only to see him leap up and send the ball flying off course. The coach of every team the Texans play is asked about how to stop Watt from making these types of plays. Most of them simply say they hope to limit the times he bats down the ball.

Even Kubiak, Houston's coach until 2013, was left searching for an answer when asked how he'd keep Watt from batting down passes if he were playing against him. "It's difficult," he said. "It's not like you can duck and throw under him and stuff like that." ★

In the October 9, 2014, divisional matchup, the Colts' Andrew tries his luck against J.J.

6 | Giving Back

Charity First

Long before he was Mega Watt or J.J. Swatt, the NFL's most feared defender, Watt was thinking about charity. He was volunteering a lot at children's hospitals and youth organizations and wanted to find a way to help more people. With an assist from his mother, Connie, he put together a plan to do just that. While still at Wisconsin he established the Justin J. Watt Foundation. The goal of the foundation is simple and close to Watt's heart.

The foundation's mission statement is: "to provide after-school opportunities for middle-school-aged children in the community to become involved in athletics, so that they may learn the character traits of accountability, teamwork, leadership, work ethic, and perseverance while in a safe and supervised environment with their peers."

Watt is the foundation's president and Connie serves as vice president and handles its day-to-day business. Jonathan Singer, a friend from Pewaukee High School, also works for the foundation as the director of operations. He reviews applications and checks out organizations and schools that request help.

When Watt first started the foundation, it didn't have much of a budget. As his celebrity has grown, so has the amount

Watt helps a young fan and aspiring pro player shop for a football during a Houston Boys & Girls Club and Houston Texans event.

Watt greets fans with fist bumps during his J.J. Watt Charity Classic softball game in Sugar Land, Texas, on May 1, 2014.

of money his foundation has been able to pump into the community. When Watt was a rookie in 2011, the foundation donated just $20,000, split between two programs. By 2013 that number had risen to more than $260,000 and the foundation helped more than 29 different youth programs, mostly in the Houston and Milwaukee areas. This year Watt's charity reached a major cumulative milestone when it surpassed the $1 million mark after doling out more than $426,000 in 2015.

"The community is huge to me," Watt said. "I want to give back as much as I can, and it's so important to me that kids get the same opportunities that I got growing up. Obviously, that's the whole basis behind my foundation.... I understand I was very fortunate growing up as a kid, and I was given many great opportunities. I don't want kids to have to suffer because adults can't afford those opportunities for them.... That's why I give back when I do."

Most of the money for the foundation has been raised by a celebrity softball game that Watt has hosted in each of the last three years. In it Watt and Houston's defenders are pitted against the team's offensive players. There is also a home-run derby, where Watt gets a chance to show off his immense power in a venue other than the football field.

Some athletes have said they don't want to be role models, and they shy away from helping children. That will never be the case with Watt, who has become exactly what the NFL needs at a time when many players are dealing with off-the-field problems. He is dedicated to being a good example for kids and helps in any way he can. He said: "You never want to see kids sad. You never want to see kids have to go through a tough time, so any chance that we can put a smile on a kid's face, even for five seconds, that's a huge deal. I love doing that, and I'll continue to do it until I'm done. We have an unbelievable platform as football players...as NFL players the world kind of looks up to us. I feel like it's our job. It's our duty to put on a good show and be a good role model for those kids and be someone that they can look up to."

Special Friends

The summer before Watt played his first game as a Texan he made a play that was bigger to one family than anything he's done on the field. The Berry family was driving home to Houston from a vacation in Colorado on July 2, 2011, when their car was hit head-on by a distracted driver. Parents Josh and Robin were killed, and their three orphaned children were left severely injured.

Little Willa was six at the time and suffered several broken bones, but eight-year-old Aaron and nine-year-old Peter were much more seriously injured. They both suffered spinal cord injuries that left them paralyzed from the waist down. Watt heard about the family and decided on his own to visit the trio in

Houston Texans offensive players Andre Johnson, Arian Foster, and Duane Brown celebrate their win against the Texans defense in the J.J. Watt Charity Classic.

the hospital a few days after the accident. Watt didn't simply stop in and say hi, never to be heard from again. From that one visit sprang a wonderful and important friendship. He called the kids, he texted with them, and after they'd recovered enough to leave the hospital, he visited them often at the home of the aunt and uncle who took them in after the accident. He was like a really, really big brother. They played basketball, hung out, and most important laughed and had a chance to escape the painful reality of what happened to them.

Pop star Justin Bieber also took notice of the plight of the Berry children and invited them and Watt to a concert in 2012. It was a celebration for Peter's birthday, and Watt got a kick out of seeing Bieber smash the cake they got for his birthday into Peter's face.

"They're just great kids," Watt said. "It's unbelievable to see their spirit. To go through what they had to go through at such a young age and see the way they bounce back, they're so lively."

Watt even gave them a visual shout-out during the Texans' November 18, 2012, game against the Jaguars. Watt fought off a block, grabbed quarterback Chad Henne, and drilled him to the ground for a six-yard loss in the fourth quarter of the overtime win. Watt quickly popped up and mimicked rolling a wheelchair, something he told the kids he'd do if he got a sack.

Peter wrote a paper about a person who inspires him, and not surprisingly that person was Watt. The young boy talked about what Watt means to him and said his motto of "Dream Big, Work Hard" has helped him since the accident. "No matter how famous or wealthy you are, everybody is equal," Peter said, reading the paper on ESPN. "I always wear his bracelet that says *DBWH*, Dream Big and Work Hard. He is the best defensive player in the NFL because he never gives up."

Watt remains close with the children to this day and keeps up with everything going on in their lives. He knows they appreciate his friendship, but he's quick to point out that they've added a special richness to his life too. "Those kids are some of the best things that have ever happened to my life, and I'm so fortunate to have them in my life," Watt said. "It's just so neat how the community, how their family and how everybody rallied around them, and to see how they responded. As you know, that's such a tough situation to be in as a child. But they handled it better than any of us could have ever imagined."

Can't Forget the Family

When Watt signed his huge contract in 2014, the first thing he wanted to do was take care of his family. He has talked often about how his parents spent their lives doing things for him and his brothers. They shuttled them to and from the football field and hockey rink, cooked them several meals a day, and sometimes missed out on things they wanted to do so they could always be there for their kids.

"Everything that they did our entire lives, they sacrificed their own time and their own ability to make sure that my brothers and I had opportunities," Watt said. "For me now to get this opportunity, for me now to be able to take care of them is honestly probably the best feeling in the world you can have as a son. I really...I

Family and friends are everything to J.J. Celebrating Draft Day, Watt is joined by (from left) Pewaukee High School head football coach Clay Iverson, brothers Derek Watt and T.J. Watt, parents Connie and John Watt, and assistant PHS coach Mike Lecher.

can't wait to be able to take care of them, to be able to tell my parents, 'Hey, if you want to do something, do it.'"

He hasn't shared everything he's done for his parents, but he did provide a personal glimpse into a special moment he had with his mother last year. On her birthday in October he surprised her with a shiny new white Range Rover adorned with a big red bow. Watt said, "I told her in the card...'Growing up on TV I saw all the commercials with red bows on them at Christmastime, and I always thought to myself, *Who can do that? Who can just buy a whole car for somebody's birthday or for Christmas and then put a bow on it in the driveway?*'" Since it was during the season, Watt wasn't there when his mother received the gift, but one of his brothers made a video of the moment so he could see her reaction.

"My whole life my parents have made sacrifices for me, and they've done everything," Watt said. "They've made it so that my brothers have had opportunities to have success. To be able to give back to her and surprise her like that...there is really no better feeling in the world than that. Just being able to take care of your family, to take care of those that are closest to you—no better way to spend my money than that." ★

Watt catches passes during the "Let Us Play" Fitness and Skills Challenge at Jacob Javits Field at George Washington High School on April 30, 2011, in New York. Players attending the NFLPA Rookie Debut put on a clinic for middle school and high school students emphasizing non-contact football skills and healthy-living habits.

7 | Money Doesn't Motivate Me, Greatness Does

Hitting Rock Bottom

Coming off two straight playoff appearances, the Texans entered the 2013 season poised to take the next step and were talked about as a Super Bowl contender. Things started out promising, with Houston winning its first two games and Watt getting two sacks and knocking down two passes in the process.

The cracks began to appear in Week 3 when Matt Schaub threw an interception that was returned for a touchdown to help the defending Super Bowl champion Ravens to a 30–9 win. Schaub's problems with accuracy continued a week later when Houston led by 17 points before the Seahawks rallied to get a 23–20 overtime win. Schaub threw two interceptions in that game, including one that Richard Sherman returned 58 yards for a score that forced overtime.

Watt sustained a deep gash on the bridge of his nose in the third quarter of that game that required six stitches to close up. He didn't miss a play because of the injury, and a trainer simply placed a bandage over the cut during the game. That didn't stop it from gushing blood every time he delivered a hit, sending red streaks streaming down his face and all over his mouth for the rest of the game. Photos of his face covered in blood from that day

Watt stays relentless, giving chase to
Titans quarterback Jake Locker.

A bloodied Watt soldiers
on against the Seahawks.

provide a lasting image of Watt and visual evidence of his intensity.

Watt didn't shower before speaking to reporters after that game. His face remained spattered with blood and his once-pristine white pants were dotted with more of the fluid that flowed from the cut on his nose. On his face sat a snarl in place of his usual sunny smile. Watt was as angry as he'd ever been since arriving in Houston.

"I'm pissed off," he said almost spitting out the words. "This sucks. Nobody likes to lose, especially like this in your own building. This isn't fun. I'm sick of it." It was a side of Watt he'd rarely shown publicly, and it conveyed just how personally he takes the team's successes and failures. "Every loss makes me angry," he said. "I can't fricking stand losing."

But that was only the beginning of the tough times for Houston that season. Schaub threw three interceptions, including one that was returned for a touchdown on the first play of the game, in Houston's 34–3 loss to San Francisco in Week 5. It was his fourth straight game with an interception returned for a score. He was injured a week later, and former University of Houston star Case Keenum got his first NFL start in Game 7. But he couldn't turn

Named a captain in November 2012, Watt is indeed a team leader.

things around, and the Texans lost their fifth consecutive game.

The nightmare season took another terrible turn in a Sunday night game on November 3, 2013, against the Colts. Houston led 21–3 when coach Gary Kubiak collapsed at halftime and was taken off the field on a stretcher and rushed to the hospital. The stunned Texans were unable to do anything in the second half and lost 27–24.

It was soon revealed that Kubiak had had a ministroke, and defensive coordinator Wade Phillips served as interim coach in a loss at Arizona. It was one of Watt's best games of the season. He had a sack and forced two fumbles, recovering both of them. He was asked how tough it was to play well but not be able to help the Texans get back on track. "Every single Sunday you're going to get my best, no matter what the record is, no matter how we're playing, because that's just the way I'm wired," Watt said. "I'm very fortunate to be in this league and in this position. But I would be lying if I told you I wasn't extremely frustrated and extremely disappointed with the way things have gone so far."

Kubiak returned after a 10-day absence and Watt and the rest of the Texans were happy to have him back and see him healthy again. "I'm happiest for him because I know that this is what he loves to do and this is his passion," Watt said. "So you're really happy that he can be out there and doing what he loves."

Watt tied a season high with two sacks in Kubiak's return game, but Houston fell to Oakland 28–23 as the skid reached eight games. Kubiak was fired on December 6, but that didn't stop the losing. When all was said and done, the Texans had dropped the final 14 games of the season to finish 2–14. It was the NFL's worst record that season and tied the 2005 season for the worst record in franchise history.

"I'm sure a lot of guys, just like me, are ready to move on and get to work in the off-season and never let this happen again," Watt said after the last game.

Watt was one of the only bright spots in the dreadful season and finished with 80 tackles and 10.5 sacks, forced four fumbles, and defensed seven passes. His work gained him a second trip to the Pro Bowl and earned him first-team All-Pro honors for the second time.

The $100 Million Man

On September 2, 2014, the Texans rewarded Watt for his years of hard work when they signed him to a six-year contract extension worth $100 million, including $51.8 million guaranteed. The deal made him the highest-paid defensive player in NFL history, eclipsing the six-year, $96 million contract with $50 million guaranteed that former Texan Mario Williams got when he signed with the Bills in 2012.

Houston general manager Rick Smith announced the deal that he said would ensure Watt would be "wreaking havoc on quarterbacks in a Houston Texans uniform for a long time."

Before signing the extension, Watt had two years left on his rookie contract that would have paid him $1.9 million in 2014 and about $7 million in 2015.

Texans owner Bob McNair joked that he was late to the press conference announcing the deal because he had to hock his wife's jewelry to pay Watt. Then he got serious. "We normally wouldn't do that at this stage," McNair said. "We just felt that his performance had been so outstanding, his attitude so great, his work ethic is such a role model for everyone on our team that we felt that he deserves special consideration." McNair continued, "He's the best defensive player in the league. We wanted him to be compensated that way, and he is."

Watt was, of course, thrilled with the extension and couldn't stop smiling as he

Watt brings fire to the Texans in every game.

spoke with reporters about the contract that will keep him in Houston until at least 2021. "From day one I wanted to stay in Houston for a long time," he said. "And I hope the people of Houston don't mind me sticking around for a little while longer, because I happen to like it here quite a bit."

Caught in a whirlwind of emotions, Watt was asked to reflect on the past few years of his life and how far he'd come. He recounted a moment from when he was delivering pizzas before he started school at Wisconsin. "I think back to my

first day when I took that job," Watt said. "And [what] the guy that was training me told me when I told him I was just there temporarily and I was going to play for the Badgers in six months. And he looked up and down and told me I was not big enough to play for the Badgers. And so, 'Hi' to that guy."

On the day he became a millionaire many times over, Watt said he still considered himself a small-town kid from Pewaukee, Wisconsin. But now that he had all that money he went on a quest to figure

out a way to spend some of it. "I Googled 'What do rich people buy?'" Watt joked. "Because I don't feel like a rich person, and I don't really try to act like a rich person, so I don't know what they buy."

The Internet's most popular search engine didn't help him out, though. "I didn't really like the stuff I saw," he said. "So I'm gonna stick with my humble lifestyle and just keep working out."

Earning the Money

After signing his huge contract, Watt remained as determined as ever to improve and help Houston win. One of the reasons the Texans offered him such a contract is because they weren't worried that he'd slack off after getting it.

"You have to base your feeling on what the future looks like based on the past," Rick Smith said. "That's a pretty good predictor of what you will have, and everything that we've seen from J.J. gives us every confidence that he will continue to work the way that he's worked and continue to be as effective...a player [as] he's been so far."

Watt gets up—way up—for a Jay Feely field goal attempt on November 10, 2013.

Watt's small-town values and solid upbringing rule how he goes about his everyday life. That's another factor that made the Texans confident in making such a huge investment in him after just three NFL seasons. He wasn't happy simply to get a big contract; he wanted to earn every dollar of it. "Money doesn't motivate me, greatness does," Watt said. "That's the truth."

Of course he appreciates having a big contract and is happy that he'll be able to take care of his family and future children. But he was most happy to get the deal done so he didn't have to think about financial stability ever again. "I'm so fortunate for all of that, that I don't have to worry about the money, so that I can focus on the greatness," he said.

After he signed the deal his parents asked him how it felt to be a multimillionaire. He shared the answer he gave them. "It feels awesome," he said he told them. "But at the end of the day, it really doesn't feel that much different, because it's not going to change who I am or the way that I live my life. I'm going to go out there every single day and chase greatness."

As he sat right next to him, McNair was asked what he thought about Watt's comments. "That's why he got the contract," McNair said with a smile. ★

Every snap brings a new battle: this one against Denver Broncos guard Orlando Franklin in Week 16.

8 | On Another Level

Watt gets Redskins quarterback Robert Griffin III
exactly where he wants him: on the ground.

Taking Over

Just six days after inking his six-year, $100 million contract extension, Watt and the Texans opened the season against the Washington Redskins. Watt promised to live up to the massive contract and earn every penny Houston gave him. And in the first game he didn't disappoint. Watt blocked an extra point, recovered a fumble, and swatted down a pass. He also harassed Robert Griffin III all day, sacking him once and hurrying him five other times.

"The goal is always to be underpaid," Watt said after that game. "You never want to be that guy that people say, 'He got money and shut down.' So I want to go out there every single day...and prove that I'm worth it."

Houston got a 17–6 win to snap the 14-game skid from the 2013 season and give new coach Bill O'Brien his first win as a head coach. Seeing Watt live on game day for the first time was certainly a treat for the coach. "Watt is obviously a hell of a football player, there's no other way to put it," O'Brien said. "He plays a lot of different spots on the line; he has the ability to disrupt the game."

Watt had another big game in Week 4 against the Buffalo Bills. With Houston's offense sputtering and the Texans trailing 10–7 in the third quarter, Watt came through once again. He threw his hands up, swatted a pass by EJ Manuel, and grabbed it for an interception. Cornerback Kareem Jackson blocked Manuel and Watt cruised 80 yards for a touchdown that gave the Texans the lead for good. Watt high-stepped his way into the end zone before waving his right hand in the air from side to side. The movement seemed to be a rendition of the then-popular dance the Nae Nae.

Watt made fun of himself after seeing the play—and ensuing dance—unfold on the Jumbotron. "I was like, 'You're a white defensive lineman, just run the ball in,'" Watt said with a laugh.

Texans owner Bob McNair was stunned by the spectacular play. "What next? I couldn't believe it," McNair said. "I just kept saying over and over again that it was unbelievable and I couldn't believe what I was seeing."

Watt also had a career-best nine hits on Manuel and five tackles against the Bills. He was so good in that game that McNair worried about what it might cost him. "He is worth every cent," McNair said. "I hope he doesn't come in tomorrow and ask for a raise."

That game wrapped up a fabulous September that earned Watt AFC Player of the Month honors. But he wasn't done yet. He was only revving up. Watt padded his highlight reel in a loss to the Colts on October 9. Houston fell behind 24–0 in the first quarter but made it close late in the game, thanks in large part to Watt. Andrew Luck fumbled early in the fourth quarter and Watt pounced on the ball. He rolled to his feet and dashed 45 yards for the score to get Houston to within five at 33–28.

"Generally, defensive linemen don't run very far," Texans defensive coordinator Romeo Crennel said. "But J.J. is a different kind of cat, so he was able to run for a touchdown when he recovered the fumble."

The Texans had two chances to take the lead after that, the second one after Watt batted down a pass by Luck on third down, but they fumbled both times. Watt finished the game with seven tackles, two sacks, three tackles for losses, three passes defensed, and four hits on Luck.

The Texans had dropped three games in a row heading into a game against Tennessee in Week 8. As usual, it was Watt who stepped up to get Houston back on track. He had two sacks, forced a fumble, swatted down a pass, and had two tackles for losses in the 30–16 win.

Watt also taught rookie Zach Mettenberger a lesson in the Tennessee quarterback's first career start. Watt saw that Mettenberger had posted some selfies on social media in the days leading up to the game, and one of them was taken only a couple hours before kickoff. After drilling Mettenberger to the ground in the fourth quarter for his second sack, Watt got up and pantomimed taking a selfie. "I take my job very seriously, and if I was a rookie quarterback and a

Watt celebrates after scoring his first touchdown of the 2014 season, against the Raiders in Week 2. It wouldn't be his last.

Another week, another TD: Watt gets six against Buffalo at home.

starter for my first time in the league, I'd be a little bit more focused than that," Watt said. "Maybe he'll learn from it, maybe not, but we won the game, and that's all that matters."

The Texans lost to the Eagles in Week 9, but Watt returned with a vengeance after a week of rest during Houston's Week 10 bye. He did a little bit of everything in the 23–7 win over the Cleveland Browns that helped the Texans improve to 5–5. He had a strip sack and five tackles, including a season-high three for losses. Watt also recovered a fumble to give him an NFL-best four for the season. It was a performance that earned him AFC Defensive Player of the Week honors.

Cleveland coach Mike Pettine raved about his work. "He's a special player," Pettine said. "You run to him. You run away from him. You try to do different things."

Ryan Fitzpatrick threw six touchdown passes to set a franchise record in a 45–21 win over Tennessee on November 30. While Fitzpatrick was the star of that victory, Watt played a major supporting role. He had two sacks, one tackle for a loss, and six quarterback hits. He forced a fumble by Jake Locker on one of his sacks and recovered it to set a franchise-record with five fumble recoveries for the season. The game gave him 11.5 sacks for the year, making him the first Texan with three seasons with at least 10 sacks.

In a 23–17 victory over Jacksonville a week later, Watt hurried and harassed quarterback Blake Bortles all day. He had three sacks, four tackles for losses—both season highs—and five quarterback hits.

Watt squashes the play—
and Tony Romo.

Watt made Texans history in a 25–13 win over the Ravens on December 21 when he sacked Joe Flacco in the fourth quarter to give him 54 career sacks and make him the team's all-time sacks leader. "It is pretty cool," Watt said about becoming Houston's sacks leader. "It is pretty neat to think sometimes that it is still early on in my career and there are some exciting things left that I would like to accomplish."

He added a season-high eight tackles, including three for losses, and four quarterback hits in the victory.

Watt and the Texans wrapped up the season with a 23–17 win over Jacksonville to make a seven-game improvement over their terrible 2013 season and finish 9–7. Not surprisingly, Watt was instrumental in this victory too. He tied a season high with three sacks and recorded his first safety of the season.

He Plays Offense Too!

In Houston's second game of 2014 Watt went back to a position he hadn't played since he was at Central Michigan in 2007. The dominant defenseman moved over to offense and lined up as a tight end. In the second week of the season, Watt slipped into the end zone as two defenders keyed in on running back Arian Foster and was wide open for a one-yard touchdown reception that gave Houston an early lead in a 30–14 win over the Raiders.

Watt tried to downplay his versatility. "If that's a way that I can help the team and continue to help the team, then I'll do that," Watt said.

Watt, who hadn't scored a touchdown on offense since high school, said he didn't lobby for the opportunity. "I thought they were teasing me when they were first talking about it, but we put it in, and it works in a game," he said. "To have a chance to score a touchdown in an NFL game on the offensive side of the ball is something that's pretty darn cool."

Watt said he felt like a little kid when he scored. The big guy received a bit of ribbing from his teammates on offense after the touchdown. Star receiver Andre Johnson, the all-time leading receiver in franchise history, was the first one to tease him. "I was joking on the sidelines, like, 'He got a touchdown before I did,'" Johnson said. "It just shows how many ways we can use him, not just defensively. He's a heck of an athlete; he's always catching balls with us on the [jug machines]. I thought they would be looking for him, but they left him open."

Watt had to wait a few weeks, but soon he was back in on offense again. In the first quarter of the aforementioned 23–7 win over the Cleveland Browns, he lined up as a tight end. Watt broke into the end zone, but this time he wasn't wide open. Linebacker Christian Kirksey stayed right with him as Ryan Mallett launched the pass into the air. But Watt used those long arms normally used for swatting down passes to reach over

Kirksey to reel in the two-yard touchdown reception.

Watt got another chance on offense in that November 30 win over the Titans. And he just might have saved his best catch for last. Watt lined up at fullback before moving out to tight end and stretching out to snag a one-yard touchdown reception from Ryan Fitzpatrick. "It was an unreal throw by Fitz," Watt said. "He put it in a spot where nobody but me could get it, and it was a perfect throw...it was just a matter of going out there and grabbing it."

McNair knew what would happen as soon as he saw Watt line up on offense. "I was thinking, *Here goes a touchdown for J.J.*," McNair said. "And it was. He made a great play."

As Watt's offensive touchdowns began to pile up, Houston receiver DeAndre Hopkins was asked if Watt was as good a receiver as him. Hopkins provided a candid answer. "No," Hopkins said. "But he makes plays, so that's all that matters. The in-between stuff isn't really a big deal if you go out and make plays. But as far as being a receiver, nah."

That doesn't mean Hopkins, a first-round pick in 2013, wasn't impressed by Watt's scores on offense. He was floored by the fact that, by the third touchdown, teams had to know the ball was going to Watt

Watt has blockers as he takes another ball to the house, this one an Andrew Luck interception.

but still couldn't keep him from scoring. "Ninety-five percent of the time you know that if J.J.'s out there, he's getting the ball; he's not going to waste his time," Hopkins said.

Watt got some pointers on catching touchdown passes from Houston assistant coach Mike Vrabel. The former linebacker also pulled double duty in his NFL career and scored a touchdown on all of his 12 career receptions. "[Vrabel] has definitely helped," Watt said. "I think that he might have helped in getting the package in the first place. He has given me some tips."

In Cleveland on November 16, Watt enjoyed his best day yet: three of his five tackles went for a loss, he forced a fumble, recovered another fumble, and caught a touchdown pass.

His work on offense, coupled with his dominance on defense, left O'Brien shaking his head. "He is definitely one of the most versatile players I've ever been around," O'Brien said. "The thing...I think that sets him apart is his work ethic, the way he approaches every single day. He's got tremendous talent, but he really does a great job of working extremely hard every day to get the most out of that talent."

What Can't This Guy Do?

Nobody in NFL history has filled up a stat sheet the way Watt did in 2014. He finished the year with 29 tackles for losses and 50 quarterback hits to lead the league in both categories. His 20.5 sacks were second in the NFL and made him the first player in NFL history to have 20 or more sacks in two seasons. He also forced four fumbles, recovered five fumbles, and had 78 tackles. Watt swatted down 10 passes to join Jason Taylor as the only players since 1991 to have at least 10 sacks and 10 passes defensed in two seasons.

And all of those statistics don't even address the scoring he did. Watt had an interception return for a touchdown, scored once on a fumble return, caught three touchdown receptions, and earned a safety to account for 32 points.

Watt was the first player in NFL history with a receiving touchdown, a fumble return for a touchdown, a safety, and an interception return for a score in a single season. He became the first defensive lineman since Chicago Bears defensive end Connie Mack Berry in 1944 to score at least five touchdowns in a season.

Watt had at least two sacks in all six of Houston's division games, and his 14 sacks within the AFC South were the most since the NFL went to a six-game division schedule when the Texans joined the league in 2002. He piled up nine sacks in the last month of the season to give him the most sacks in December since 1982.

O'Brien, who normally doesn't gush about anything, couldn't help but lavish praise on Watt at the end of the season. "The guy is a fantastic football player," O'Brien said. "He disrupts the play on every play. If you sat down and watched the tape of him and really studied the game, the guy really affects every single play of a game. To me, I look like I'm 60 years old, but I'm only 45 and I haven't been around long enough to say if he's the best of all time and all those things, but I can tell you in my time in the league, I've never seen a defensive player like him that affects the play on every play." ★

9 | MVP Candidate

Watt shows tenacity and intensity on every play.

He Deserves It

Watt's spectacular 2014 season was the toast of the NFL. Teammates, players around the league, coaches, and commentators alike were all in awe of the things Watt did each and every week. There was no doubt he was the best defensive player in the league, but many believed he had also made a strong case to be the league's MVP.

Watt had three sacks and a safety in Houston's season finale against Jacksonville. After the game, teammate Andre Johnson summed up what many thought about Watt's season. "If he doesn't win the MVP," Johnson said, "the NFL is out of their mind."

Houston receiver DeAndre Hopkins agreed and compared Watt to fellow front-runner Green Bay quarterback Aaron Rodgers. "Aaron Rodgers doesn't sack quarterbacks and catch touchdowns," Hopkins said. "[Watt's] multitalented. When's the last time you've seen a defensive end with this many touchdowns [who is] able to make the catches he's made?"

Obviously Watt's teammates would be rooting for him to be named the NFL's best overall player. But it wasn't just the Texans who were convinced he should win MVP. Seattle linebacker Bruce Irvin was asked who should win the award in the days leading up to the Super Bowl. "Obviously, J.J. Watt," he told reporters. "He's a freak.... [He's] a defensive guy doing that stuff. You expect that from Tom Brady; he's a Hall of Famer. But you got a [defensive lineman] and he's got 20 sacks, five touchdowns; come on, that's unheard of."

Colts coach Chuck Pagano, who had to game plan for Watt twice that season, discussed how difficult he was to deal with. "Like a quarterback touches the ball every single play, J.J. affects the game that way,"

Pagano said. "I know he doesn't play that position. You normally don't see it from a position at the defensive line, but he's as good as or better than anybody that's ever played on that side of the football, and his numbers speak for themselves and he affects [the game] in so many ways."

Late in the season Pagano had made up his mind who the league's best player was. "He's a nightmare," Pagano said. "He's

Quarterbacks fear him, offensive linemen can't stop him.

It's not just the swat; Watt catches and runs too.

damn near unblockable...he'd get my vote for MVP right now."

Watt deflected questions about the award all season, always preferring to talk about the team instead. On the day after the season ended, Watt was again pressed about whether he thought he had a chance to win MVP. "I left everything I had out there on that field trying to help my team win, doing whatever I could to be the best football player that I could be," he said. "However they want to vote, whatever they want to write, they can write whatever they want, but I know that I left it all out there."

He insisted that he doesn't worry about things out of his control, instead focusing on how much he loves playing the game and the joy it can bring people. "You can quantify greatness however you want, but for me it's knowing that somebody's in their living room watching the game that I've never met, and they'll never meet me, but they get a smile when I make a play," Watt said. "And that's one of the best feelings in the whole world."

Bias Against Defense

Despite Watt's amazing season, many were convinced he wouldn't win the award simply because he plays defense. In the history of the award, which was first given in 1957, a defender has only won it twice. The first defensive player to pick up the hardware

And he scores touchdowns.

was Minnesota tackle Alan Page, in 1971. New York Giants linebacker Lawrence Taylor joined him as the only other defensive winner when he won it in 1986. Both are in the Hall of Fame.

Texans veteran cornerback Johnathan Joseph noted the perceived bias against defensive players when talking about Watt's season. "After a performance like that and a year like he's had, if he [doesn't] get the MVP, I don't think any year a defensive player should ever be capable of getting it, because I don't think you can top that performance," Joseph said.

Baltimore linebacker Terrell Suggs thought the fact that Watt scored five touchdowns would help his MVP case, but lamented that quarterbacks have an automatic leg up on the competition. "In the world we live in, people want to see touchdowns. People are big fans of quarterbacks," Suggs said. "It's just our game. They like touchdowns. Unfortunately, we are the defensive guys. But he has [touchdowns], so he's definitely in the argument."

Despite Watt's record-setting season, Rodgers was named the MVP for the second time. Watt came in second with 13 out of 50 votes. It was the most votes a defensive player had received since 1999. The award has been given to a quarterback 37 times,

The Houston faithful make a good point.

and running backs are second, picking it up in 18 seasons.

Rodgers was asked about Watt's chances of ever winning the award soon after he picked up his MVP trophy. "Well, it's tough, to be honest with you," Rodgers said. "He knows that it's an offensive-geared league and a quarterback or a running back usually wins this award. It's probably tough, but I think if anybody can do it, it's him."

Though he came up short in MVP voting, Watt got support from one of the two defenders who have won the award. Before the 2015 season began, Taylor told *Sports Illustrated* that Watt "should have been MVP."

Two-Time Winner

Watt lost out to Rodgers for MVP but got a nice consolation prize in the form of his second Defensive Player of the Year Award. He became the first unanimous selection for the honor, gaining all 50 votes from the nationwide panel of media members who regularly cover the league.

"I'm proud to represent my teammates, coaches, the organization, and the city of Houston," Watt said. "So many people helped make this award possible. It's a testament to everyone from my elementary school teachers to teammates and coaches."

On any given Sunday, 99 seems to be Houston's lucky number.

He became the sixth player to win the award twice, joining Bruce Smith, Reggie White, Mike Singletary, Joe Greene, and Ray Lewis in the elite group.

Watt was also named to his third Pro Bowl and was selected as an All-Pro for the third season. ★

10 | A Bright and Still-Rising Star

Watt takes in an NCAA basketball game with tennis star Caroline Wozniacki.

Meeting the Girl of His Dreams

Watt has said repeatedly that he doesn't have time for a special lady in his life because football keeps him so busy. However, there is one woman who could wrestle him away from the sport he loves so much. He's had a crush on Jennifer Aniston for as long as he can remember, and this summer his dream came true when he got to meet the movie star. "It was incredible," Watt told the Associated Press. "She was very sweet."

He posted a picture of the two of them on Instagram with the caption, "I'm not even going to try to pretend like I acted cool when this happened. #LifeMade."

Watt knew that Aniston was engaged at the time and has since married fellow actor Justin Theroux. But he still thought about trying to put a ring on her beautiful finger. "I shook her hand instead of hugging her," he said, joking. "Then I left the room without proposing. It was a complete disaster."

Though meeting Aniston was the highlight of his off-season, she was far from the only celebrity Watt rubbed elbows with. He starred in a Reebok commercial with UFC star Ronda Rousey, spent time with Arnold Schwarzenegger, and met NBA star Kevin Durant, actress Eva Longoria, and model Kathy Ireland.

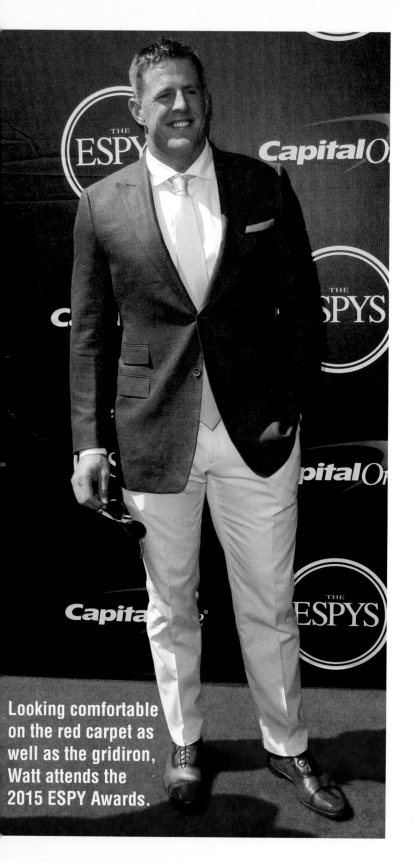

Looking comfortable on the red carpet as well as the gridiron, Watt attends the 2015 ESPY Awards.

He joked that he wouldn't even try to fight Rousey, saying she's one of the baddest people on the planet. "I have a lot of respect for what she does and how hard she works, so it's been fun to be able to kind of get to know her and connect with her a bit," Watt said.

He caused a stir when he took in an NCAA tournament game with tennis star Caroline Wozniacki, but never confirmed the two were a pair. So for now he remains Houston's most eligible bachelor.

"Just the opportunities that I've been given and the experiences I've gotten to have are truly unbelievable," Watt said of his star-studded off-season. "It's really neat and really special to be able to see the things I've seen, meet the people I meet, have the conversations I've had. So it's been crazy and it's been fun. I said this year one of those things I was trying to work on is making sure that I enjoyed everything that comes with this, so I'm trying to do that."

Of course Watt didn't let his globe-trotting interfere with his off-season workouts and brought his trainer with him when he visited Los Angeles. "The training was never impeded by any of it, and I think that's what's the most important to me," he said. "When I was out in L.A. for that whole week my trainer was out there with me, and I'm thankful to him for that, because like I said, the reason I am where I am today is because of the work that's been put in and the reason that I'm hopefully going to continue to have that success is because of the work that's continuing to be put in."

Just before training camp began in 2015 Watt was back in Houston and took some time out to visit Minute Maid Park and catch up with a few baseball players. Watt met Astros stars Carlos Correa, Jose Altuve, and Dallas Keuchel and also spent time with Los Angeles Angels star Mike Trout, the 2014 American League MVP.

"It was pretty cool. He's probably the best player in baseball, and he's a real nice guy as well," Watt said of Trout. "We've texted back and forth before but never actually met, so it was nice to get a chance to meet him. It's always nice to be able to connect with people in other sports who are doing big things and doing things the right way."

The only drawback to dabbling in a celebrity lifestyle in the off-season was that it took time away from the low-key way he usually spends his time off. "I would have liked more time to just hang

Watt threw out the Astros' first pitch on Opening Day in 2015.

Watt shares more rarefied air—this time at the White House Correspondents' Dinner in 2014, which he attended with his mother, Connie.

out with my family and friends," he said. "I think I got a lot of that time. I did. And when we did get it, it was awesome. That's the one thing every single year...I really, really enjoy just quiet nights with family and friends, just hanging out around the bonfire."

And He Acts

Watt's celebrity took another turn when he moved from the football field to the small screen in 2013, appearing as himself in three episodes of FX's comedy *The League*. Poking fun at his own image as well as the slavish devotion fantasy football players give to their pastime, he displayed expert comic timing alongside the show's cast.

Then in March 2015, he took a part on the hit FOX sitcom *New Girl*. His role didn't require all that much acting, since he played himself yet again. Regardless, he looked comfortable and cool as he shared the screen with the cast that includes Zooey Deschanel and Damon Wayans Jr. The comedic performance was capped with the three of them singing a silly song about hot dogs. The best part about it was that we learned that among Watt's many talents, he can also carry a tune.

Building His Brand

Watt has skyrocketed to a level of fame no other defensive lineman in the history of the game has had. He's now piling up endorsement deals, magazine covers, and other perks that have in the past been reserved for quarterbacks and running backs.

His sponsorship agreements include Reebok, Gatorade, H-E-B, Verizon, Ford, and NRG. According to Forbes, he earns $7 million from endorsements, which is $5 million more than any other defensive player in the league.

His commercials with Verizon and NRG have helped vault his fame to another echelon. Those spots are also fun and give him a chance to show a softer side. The man who makes his money terrorizing quarterbacks enjoyed showing off his dance moves at a junior high dance in a Verizon commercial last year. And in the summer of 2015 a new batch of commercials for NRG had Watt involved in synchronized swimming and curling.

In 2013 Watt, who often seems superhuman on the field, was transformed into a superhero in a DC comic book. Watt became Mega Watt in the book, which was sponsored by Gatorade and told an abbreviated version of his life story.

The Watt train keeps chugging along.

Watt with a hand on the football is already a familiar sight.

"You kind of dream about being a superhero or things like that," Watt said. "To see myself [in] a comic book, and to see my entire story there, it's really cool and it's definitely something that...helps get a message across to kids that if you dream big and work hard you can do anything you want."

Watt enjoyed shooting covers for a variety of magazines in the past year.

He appeared on the front of *ESPN the Magazine* with pop star Katy Perry and also graced the covers of *Sports Illustrated* and *Texas Monthly*. Then there was the cover of *Men's Health*, which had women across the country swooning. On it the almost-300-pound Watt is wearing football pants and is shirtless, giving everyone an eyeful of his perfectly defined six-pack abs.

He posted a pic of that cover on Instagram and joked in the caption about what it took to look like that. "I'm not going to lie, I am flexing my abs as hard as a 290-pound man possibly can in this new @MensHealthMag cover," he wrote.

He also posted a behind-the-scenes video of the shoot and said that he was channeling a character from the 2001 comedy film about male models called *Zoolander*. "It's pretty cool," he said. "At some point, you kind of got to turn into that Derek Zoolander–type moment. I don't know if I hit Magnum or not. It was worth a shot."

What's Next for Watt?

Just before the start of the 2015 season NFL players voted Watt No. 1 on the list of the top 100 players that the NFL Network puts out each year.

Of course, getting such an honor didn't change anything for the bright and still-rising star. "They know how hard we all work, so for them to name me No. 1 was incredible," he said. "But then it's also motivating, because I want to go out there and prove that I'm worthy of that title. I want to go out there and prove to these guys and to everybody that I work my [butt] off to be great."

At just 26 and only four seasons into his career, Watt has already done things unheard of for a defensive lineman, set numerous records, and picked up two Defensive Player of the Year awards. Yet Watt is nowhere close to being satisfied, and as the 2015 season approached, he shared the ridiculously high expectations he has for himself. "It's not necessarily some sort of quantifiable award or numbers or things like that," Watt said. "It's, *Am I better today than I was yesterday?* Then it becomes, *Am I better this year than I was last year?* It's just every single day finding something to improve upon."

Watt said he attacks each practice, workout, and film study with the same intensity he brings to games. "If I don't do that, then I failed myself and then that's where we start to have problems," he said. "It's not like I want to get this many this, or I want to do this or that and get these awards, it's just go out there and be the best possible football player that you can be every single day and continually improve." He thought for a second before continuing, "I don't know where that takes me, I don't know how high it can go, but my goal is to see how far we can push it." ✪